ALWAYS ANGELS

OVER 20 EASY-TO-MAKE CREATIVE HOLIDAY PROJECTS

TABLE OF CONTENTS

Photography—Brian Birlauf

Setups—Helen Hall

Illustrations and Graphics—Marilyn Robinson and Lynn Pike

Editing—Sharon Holmes

© 1991 Lynda Milligan and Nancy Smith

Published in the United States of America by "Possibilities," Denver, Colorado.

Library of Congress Catalog Card Number: 9160696

ISBN: 0-9622477-5-8

First Printing 1991

TOOLS AND SUPPLIES

Acrylic Paints - (for the wood projects in this book) a water-based paint available in a variety of sizes and a large color range.

Bandbox Kit - round, oval, hexagonal or heart-shaped, die-cut cardboard pieces for making one complete box including lid. Cardboard pieces are covered with wallpaper, wrapping paper, or fabric and are sometimes lightly padded. Pieces are glued or sewn together.

Contact Paper or Laminating Film - permanent, self-adhesive, protective film. Brands: Contact, Coverseal.

Fabric Paints - plastic tubes of paint available in a wide range of colors and sizes. They are permanent, non-toxic, dry-cleanable, and washable. Some brand names are Tulip, Polymark, and Scribbles.

Fusing Web - paper-backed bonding agent which is released by ironing. It is used to secure fabric to paper, cardboard, wood, plastic, metal, or another fabric. It is sold by the yard or in prepackaged sizes in craft and fabric stores. Brand names are Trans-Web, Heat and Bond, and Wonder-Under.

Glitterstik - a clear, oil-based marker that contains glitter. It is easy to use, is non-messy, and no glue or brushes are needed. It works like a crayon; the user can draw glitter right from the stick onto porous or nonporous surfaces such as fabric, paper, leather or painted wood.

Glue Gun - an electric gun used to melt sticks of glue. An instant bond is created. Guns can be manual or equipped with a finger trigger. Colored glue is also available.

Lamé fabric - an ornamental fabric in which metallic threads are woven with silk or rayon threads.

Needlepunch/Fleece - 100% polyester, batting-like product used to add dimension to quilted and padded crafts, home decorating projects, and garments. It does not stretch like traditional batting and is easy to cut, shape and handle.

Stationery - undecorated paper sheets and envelopes sold individually or by the pound in stationery, gift, or card stores.

ANGELIC PROJECTS

MEMORIES PHOTO ALBUM COVER

(11 1/2" x desired width and depth) Pictured on page 13.

Yardage and Supplies
Fabric (42" - 45"):
   Binder cover - 7/8 yard
   Head and arms - scrap at least 4 1/2" square
   Dress - scrap at least 6" square
   Wings, trees, stars - 1/6 yard gold lamé
Needlepunch - 1/2 yard
Paper-backed fusing web - 1/4 yard
Thread to match cover fabric
Fine permanent marking pens - red and brown
Red pencil or powder blush
Glitter paint such as Tulip Paint Writer - gold
Adhesive glitter such as Glitterstik - gold
Template plastic
3-ring binder 11 1/2" high (binder must turn back on itself at each side of spine)
Photo album insert pages for binder

To Make Album Cover:
1. Cut fabric piece 45" x the height of the binder plus 3".
2. Lay fabric right side down on table; lay needlepunch on top. Place open binder in center. Wrap ends of fabric/needlepunch over ends of binder. 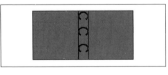 Trim ends of fabric/needlepunch to about 2/3 of the way from folded edge to rings (1/3 of inside of front and back of binder should not be covered with fabric/needlepunch). Unfold ends and remove binder.

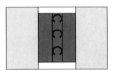

3. Bind short ends of fabric/needlepunch rectangle with strips of fabric cut 2 3/4" wide. Fold strips in half wrong sides together and pin raw edges of binding strips even with raw edges of fabric/needlepunch rectangle on the right side. Stitch in 3/8" seam. Fold to back so folded edge of binding reaches a bit past the stitching line. Pin from **right** side. Machine stitch from right side "in the ditch" catching folded edge of binding on the underside.

4. Lay binder cover (fabric/needlepunch rectangle) on table fabric side up. Center open binder on it and wrap bound ends over binder. Mark position of each bound edge on cover with pencil or pins. Slide binder out leaving folded edges of cover in place.

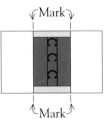

5. Cut a facing the same height as the cover by the width of the space between the bound edges plus 2". (Example: Binder is 11 1/2" tall, and you cut the cover 14 1/2" tall, so you also cut the facing 14 1/2" tall. The space between bound edges is 9", so you cut the facing 11" wide. Facing = 11" x 14 1/2".) Lay facing right side down on top of the space between the bound edges centering it and making sure bound edges are covered by facing. Pin.

6. To mark top and bottom seamlines, lay open binder on top of cover centered from top to bottom. Mark with a pencil next to top and bottom of binder. Slide binder to right and left keeping it aligned with pencil marks and mark seamlines on out to folded edges. Remove binder.

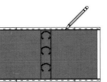

Mark and Stitch

7. Stitch a scant 1/8" *outside* each of the marked seamlines (toward top and bottom cut edges). Trim to within 1/2" of seamlines. Turn cover being sure to turn facing to inside.

8. Cut, bond, and embellish angel and stars following steps 2 through 7 of String of Stars Tree Skirt, page 17, omitting references to angel placement. Angel's arms are placed in up position. Use photo as a guide for placement. Use Glitterstik around edges of lamé stars.

9. Turn binder back on itself at each side of spine and insert both edges simultaneously into cover. Fit should be snug.

10. Fill album with wonderful memories!

PAINTED ANGEL IN GRAPEVINE WREATH

(12") Pictured on page 12.

Supplies
12" grapevine wreath
1" wood stars - approximately 12
1/2" wood stars - 3 (for standing angel in photo)
3/4" thick pine board - 10" x 10" (makes one angel)
Minwax Stain - #230 Early American
Polyfoam brush or rag for applying stain
Acrylic paints:
    Delta Ceramcoat Burgundy - dress
    Folk Art Skintone - face and arms
    Folk Art Parrot Green - trees
    Accent Summersand #2501 - wings
    DecoArt Glorious Gold - stars
Synthetic brushes in several small sizes for applying paint
Fine permanent marking pen - brown - Niji or Pigma
Krylon Matte Finish Spray Coating - #1311
Tracing paper
Graphite transfer paper (gray)
Small evergreen sprigs - halos
Glue gun and glue sticks

To Make Angel Wreath:
1. Cut angel from pine board using outline of pattern on page 24.
2. Sand angel. Apply sealer to front of angel only.
3. Stain sides and back of angel.
4. Trace pattern from book, page 24, onto tracing paper. Transfer pattern to wood angel using graphite transfer paper (used the same way as carbon paper).
5. Paint angel starting with face and arms. Paint wings and dress. Paint trees last if doing standing angel adding dotted lines with tiny brush. Paint tops and sides of small stars. Paint star attached to angel's hand.
6. Outline angel and add detail to wings and face using permanent pen. Use photo as a guide.
7. Use small, stiff brush to apply cheeks using the dry brush technique. Dab brush in burgundy paint and then on paper towel to remove most of the paint. Test before using by pouncing on towel. Apply to cheeks by pouncing lightly.

8. For angel with larger gold stars on dress, glue stars to dress and finish dress by painting gold dots above and below stars. For angel with trees on dress, glue small gold stars above trees.

9. Spray several light coats of spray coating over entire angel letting dry between coats.

10. Glue angel and stars to wreath. Add their evergreen halos.

11. Hang your wreath and enjoy!

TRIM-A-TREE PLACEMAT

(13" x 18") Fun for children as well as adults! Pictured on page 15.

Yardage and Supplies (makes one placemat)
Fabric (42" - 45"):
    Head and arms - scrap at least 4 1/2 " square
    Dress - scrap at least 6" square
    Wings - scrap at least 3" square
Paper-backed fusing web - 1/4 yard
Fine permanent marking pens - red and brown
Red pencil or powder blush
Template plastic
Permanent lettering pen - gold - optional
Colored posterboard - 13" x 18"
Laminating film or contact paper - 16" x 40" or 1 1/8 yards
Red ribbon - 5/8 yard of 1/8" wide
1" gold sequin snowflakes - at least three for hair/halo, more if wanted as tree decorations
Stickers - small assortment of holiday stickers such as stars, presents, holly, toys, hearts, words, etc.
Glue gun and glue sticks or thick, tacky glue

To Make Placemat:
1. Cut posterboard 13" x 18". To give placemat rounded corners, draw around curved edge of a cup, glass or other round object. Trim and set aside.
2. Make templates of wing, arms, head, dress, and tree, page 21.
3. Using templates, trace patterns onto smooth, paper side of fusing web. Trace one of each pattern piece. **Remember to trace patterns the *reverse* of the direction wanted.**
4. Press fusing web to **wrong** side of desired fabric with rough side facing fabric. Cut out shapes. With pencil, lightly transfer face markings.
5. Peel off paper; arrange tree and angel on posterboard as shown in photo. If making more than one placemat, position and direction of angel and tree can be varied. Layer the angel putting down head, wing, and left arm first. Add dress covering wing, neck, and arm edges. Add remaining arm on top of dress matching edges. When design is pleasing, press with a dry iron.
6. For angel face, use permanent marking pens, brown for eyes and red for mouth. Use side of red pencil lead to blush cheeks or use powder blush.
7. To make halo/hair, glue three gold snowflakes to head.
8. Glue red ribbon to tree for garland.
9. Decorate tree, angel, and remaining placemat with a variety of stickers.
10. If desired, personalize the placemat by putting a name in the corner using the gold lettering pen, or write a special message such as "Season's Greetings", "Noel" or "Peace".
11. Cut two pieces of laminating film at least 14" x 19". Lay film side down on flat surface. Peel off paper backing. Carefully *flip placemat over* and gently center it right side down on sticky side of film. Turn

over and smooth film using a straight edge such as a ruler to remove any tucks or bubbles. Repeat process for back of placemat.

12. Trim edges of laminating film even with posterboard.
13. Set the table for a holiday meal!

ANGEL WRAPPING PAPER

Pictured on page 12.

Yardage and Supplies

Fabric (42" - 45"):
    Head and arms - scrap at least 4 1/2" square
    Dress - scrap at least 6" square
    Wings - scrap at least 3 1/2" x 5 1/2"
    Stars - scrap of gold lamé 6"square
    Trees - scrap at least 3" x 6"
Paper-backed fusing web - 1/4 yard
Brown Kraft paper - piece large enough to wrap desired package
Package ribbon - enough for desired package
Glitterpaint such as Tulip Paint Writer - gold
Adhesive glitter such as Glitterstik - gold
Fine permanent marking pens - red and brown
Red pencil or powder blush

To Make Wrapping Paper:

1. Wrap desired package with brown Kraft paper. Crease all edges but do not tape. After all edges are creased, unwrap package and lay paper out flat defining top surface area.
2. Follow directions for Hallelujah Angel Picture steps 2 through 8, page 18, omitting the small star and references to fabric background. Outline head, wings, dress, trees, and stars with glitter paint. Use Glitterstik in areas around stars and angel.
3. Re-wrap package along fold lines. Tape edges closed. Decorate with package ribbon.

CHRISTMAS STOCKING

(17") Pictured on page 10.

Yardage and Supplies

Fabric (42" - 45"):
    Stocking - 1/2 yard (3/4 yard will do both
        stocking and lining)
    Stocking lining - 1/2 yard
    Binding - 1/3 yard lamé
    Head and arms - scrap at least 4 1/2" square
    Dress - scrap at least 6" square
    Wings - scrap at least 3 1/2" x 5 1/2"
    Stars - scraps of red and green lamé at least 4"
        square each
Needlepunch - 1/2 yard
Paper-backed fusing web - 1/4 yard
Featherweight fusible interfacing (if using lamé as binding) - 1/3 yard
Fine permanent marking pens - red and brown
Red pencil or powder blush
Glitter paint such as Tulip Paint Writer - gold
Thread to match binding fabric
Gold star garland - 9"

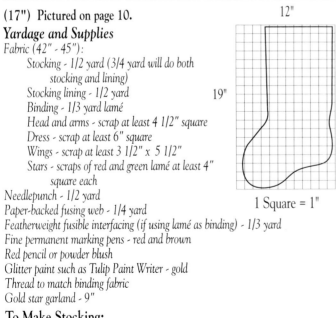
12"
19"
1 Square = 1"

To Make Stocking:

1. Enlarge pattern for stocking from grid. Cut two stockings from fabric placed wrong sides together. Repeat for two linings. Cut two of needlepunch.

2. Cut, bond, and embellish angel and stars using steps 2 through 7 of String of Stars Tree Skirt on page 17 omitting references to angel placement. Refer to photo for placement. Angel's arms are in up position. Use two sizes of stars and place them as desired. Have toe of stocking point to left.
3. Prepare a strip of bias binding 2" wide and 68" long. If using lamé for binding, bond it with featherweight interfacing before cutting.
4. Layer stocking pieces as follows with all toes pointing to left. First set: stocking back right side down, needlepunch, one lining right side up. Second set: other lining right side down, needlepunch, stocking front right side up. Pin edges.
5. Using binding in a single layer, bind top edge of each layered set. Lay raw edge of binding to right side of top edge of stocking and stitch in a 3/8" seam. Fold binding to back, tuck in raw edge, and handstitch folded edge to stitching line.
6. Pin the two sets together right sides of lining facing. Bind long curved raw edge of stocking as described above. Fold binding in on itself at each top corner for a clean finish.
7. If desired, fold and stitch a piece of binding fabric into a narrow strip to be formed into a loop and tacked to stocking for a hanger.
8. Cut a 9" piece of star garland and glue or tack into place between angel's hands.
9. Hang stocking by the fireplace for Santa to fill!

CALICO AND BUTTONS ANGEL QUILT

(46" x 66" - 10" Block) Pictured on page 16 and back cover.

Yardage and Supplies

Fabric (42" - 45"):
    Background - 3 yards (includes borders cut crosswise)
    Multicolored squares - scraps to total at least 2/3 yard
    Backing - 3 yards (pieced horizontally)
    Binding - 5/8 yard
    Head and arms - 1/6 yard
    Dress - 8 different scraps at least 6" square
    Wings - 1/4 yard
Batting - 2 yards of 48" wide or 72" x 90" prepackaged
Paper-backed fusing web - 1 yard
Thread to match background
Fine permanent marking pens - red and brown
Red pencil or powder blush
Buttons - 32 "old, collector-type", 3/8" to 5/8"
Embroidery floss - brown variegated or 2 complimentary shades of brown - 3 skeins
Template plastic

To Make Quilt:

(Use 1/4" seam allowance unless otherwise noted.)

1. Cut from background fabric:
    4 at 6 1/2" x 6 1/2" - F
    20 at 2 1/2" x 4 1/2" - G
    58 at 2 1/2" x 2 1/2" - H
    38 at 2 1/2" x 6 1/2" - I
    6 at 6 1/2" x 10 1/2" - J
    8 at 10 1/2" x 10 1/2" - K
    Borders - cut 6 at 2 1/2" x width of fabric

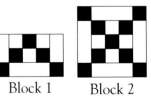
Block 1   Block 2

2. The edge of this quilt is composed of Piece J and Block 1 alternating. Piece F finishes off each corner. The inner portion of the quilt is composed of Piece K and Block 2 alternating.

a. Make 10 Block 1: Sew center section of two rows of H. Add G to each side. Sew H to each end of I. Add H/I unit to H/G unit.

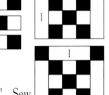

b. Make 7 Block 2: Sew center section of three rows of H. Add I to each side. Sew H to each end of I two times and add to top and bottom of center section.

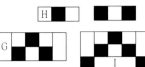

c. Assemble blocks. See quilt diagram.

3. Cut two pieces of border strips 2 1/2" x 42 1/2". Sew short ends of remaining strips together and cut two pieces 2 1/2" x 66 1/2". Sew the two shorter pieces to top and bottom of quilt. Sew the two longer pieces to the sides. Press well..

4. Set quilt top aside momentarily and prepare angels.

5. Make templates of dress, wing, head, and arms, page 23.

6. Trace patterns onto smooth, paper side of fusing web. Remember to trace two arms with one reversed.

7. Press fusing web to **wrong** side of desired fabric with rough side facing fabric. Cut out shapes. Lightly transfer face markings with a pencil.

8. Peel off paper. Position each angel on a plain 10" block. Place angel centered on block from left to right and have bottom of angel dress about 1" from bottom seamline. Layer wings first then arms and head; lay on dress overlapping neck and arm edges. Press in place.

9. Using permanent marking pens, draw mouth in red and eyes in brown. Use side of red pencil lead to blush cheeks or use powder blush. Use the brown pen to outline wings and add extra texture lines.

10. Using six-strand embroidery floss (either variegated or two shades mixed), work cross-stitches around outside of head from ear level on one side to ear level on the other side.

11. Sew four buttons evenly spaced down the front of each angel dress.

12. Seam backing fabric horizontally and trim to make a piece 50" x 70".

13. Layer backing wrong side up, then batting, and then quilt top right side up. Machine or hand quilt referring to quilt diagram and photo. Trim backing and batting even with quilt top.

14. For binding cut six strips 2 1/2" x fabric width. Sew ends together to make two strips the length of sides of quilt. Make two strips the length of the top and bottom plus 1". Press strips in half lengthwise wrong sides together. To apply, pin binding to front of quilt along both sides with raw edges even. Stitch with a 3/8" seam allowance. Wrap binding to back of quilt at four corners and pin in place. Pin and stitch binding to top and bottom edges of quilt as above but allow binding to extend 1/2" at each end. Turn extended ends of binding in before turning binding to back of quilt. Handstitch folded edge of binding to back of quilt at stitched line.

STAINED ANGEL CHEESE BOX

(9" diameter) Pictured on page 10.

Supplies
9" round wood cheese box
Minwax Stain - #230 Early American
Polyfoam brush or rag for applying stain
Windsor and Newton Colourless Art Masking Fluid
Small, stiff brush for applying masking fluid
Krylon Matte Finish Spray Coating - #1311
Fine permanent marking pen - brown - Niji or Pigma
Tracing paper
Graphite transfer paper (gray)
Drafting tape to hold pattern in place

To Decorate Cheese Box:
1. Sand cheese box.
2. Trace pattern from book, page 20, onto tracing paper.
3. Transfer pattern to box top using graphite transfer paper (used the same way as carbon paper).
4. Apply masking fluid to areas where you don't want stain to appear. See photo. Let dry.
5. Apply stain over top and bottom of cheese box. Wipe down and let dry.
6. When dry to touch, rub off masking fluid using your fingers (it feels like rubber cement). Unstained areas will appear.
7. Outline with permanent brown marker using photo as a guide. Also use pen to add facial features.
8. When dry, spray several light coats of matte finish spray coating over entire top and bottom of box. Let dry between coats.
9. Optional - box may be lined with fabric.
10. Use your special box to store sewing notions, jewelry, or other treasures.

RUFFLED PILLOW

(14" square) Pictured on page 14.

Yardage and Supplies
Fabric (42" - 45"):
    Ruffle and pillow backing - 1 yard
    Red border - 1/4 yard
    Muslin background - 1/2 yard
    Head and arms - scrap at least 4 1/2" square
    Dress - scrap at least 6" square
    Wings - scrap at least 3 1/2" x 5 1/2"
    Stars and moon - scrap at least 5" square
    Trees - scrap at least 3" x 6"
Thread to match ruffle, background

Piece F | Block 1 | Piece J

Piece K | Block 2

Piece J

Machine embroidery threads to match applique fabrics plus brown for hair
Polyester stuffing - 1 lb.
Paper-backed fusing web - 1/4 yard
Sewing stabilizer such as Stitch-N-Tear - 1/3 yard
Fine permanent marking pens - red and brown
Red pencil or powder blush
Template plastic

To Make Pillow:

(Use 1/4" seam allowance unless otherwise noted.)

1. Cut one piece of fabric 14 1/2" square for pillow backing. Cut one piece of muslin 11 1/2" square. Cut two side borders of red fabric 2" x 11 1/2". Cut two red borders 2" x 14 1/2" for top and bottom. Cut three pieces of fabric for ruffle 5 1/2" x width of fabric.

2. Make pillow top by sewing two shorter red strips to sides of muslin square. Stitch longer red strips to top and bottom.

3. Make templates of wing, dress, head, arm, trees, stars, and moon, page 20.

4. Using templates, trace patterns onto smooth, paper side of fusing web. Remember to trace two arms with one reversed. Trace 11 stars.

5. Press fusing web to **wrong** side of desired fabric with rough side facing fabric. Cut out shapes. With pencil, lightly transfer face markings. Peel off paper. Position angel on muslin square centering her from side to side and having her about 1 1/2" from the bottom of the square. Lay down wings first then head and arms. Lay down dress overlapping neck and arm edges. Add trees, stars, and moon. When the design is pleasing, press in place. Use photo as a guide.

6. To machine applique, begin by placing a piece of sewing stabilizer behind background fabric. Use a very short stitch length and a 1/16" to 1/8" wide zig-zag stitch width. Loosen top tension as needed to keep bobbin thread from being visible on top of work. Keep the threads of the satin stitch at right angles to the edge of the applique by pivoting as needed. (To pivot, leave needle in fabric, lift presser foot, turn fabric, lower foot, resume sewing.) To make tapered points, reduce stitch width while sewing. To tie off threads, bring stitch width to zero and take six to eight stitches next to the line of satin stitching. Tear away stabilizer.

7. To stitch grapevine wreath halo, machine applique a couple of squiggly lines in brown thread from ear level on one side of head to ear level on the other side varying width of stitching line as you sew.

8. Using permanent marking pens, draw eyes in brown and mouth in red. Use side of red pencil lead to blush cheeks or use powder blush.

9. To make ruffle for pillow, begin by seaming ends of strips together to make one continuous fabric loop. Press loop in half lengthwise right side out. Run two rows of gathering stitches along raw edge inside the 1/4" seam allowance. Fold ruffle into quarters and mark quarter points. With right sides together and raw edges even, pin ruffle to pillow top matching corners to quarter markings. Pull up gathers evenly allowing a little extra fullness at corners. Baste in place.

10. With right sides of top and back together, stitch around outer edge of pillow catching ruffle in stitching and leaving an opening along one side for turning. Trim corners, turn, and stuff firmly. Whipstitch opening closed.

11. Place pillow on a couch or chair and enjoy!

TRIO OF ANGELS BANNER

(16" x 30") Pictured on page 11.

Yardage and Supplies

Fabric (42" - 45"):
  Background - 2/3 yard
  Backing - 5/8 yard
  Binding - 1/4 yard
  Head and arms - 1/8 yard
  Dress - 3 different solid scraps at least 6" square each
  Wings, halos, stars - 1/4 yard gold lamé
  Dress scallop trim - scraps at least 2" x 5" of 3 colors of lamé
Batting - 18" x 32"
Fine permanent marking pens - red and brown
Red pencil or powder blush
Thread to match background
Paper-backed fusing web - 1/2 yard
Featherweight fusible interfacing - 3/8 yard
Template plastic
Optional - 1" plastic rings or sequin pins for hanging

To Make Banner:

(Use 1/4" seam allowance unless otherwise noted.)
Cut of navy:
  16 at 2" x 2" - A
  12 at 2" x 7 1/2" - B
  6 at 2" x 10 1/2" - C
  3 at 7 1/2" x 10 1/2" - D

Note: Before cutting lamé for pieced stars, bond the fusible interfacing to the back side of the lamé to stabilize it.

Cut of gold lamé:
  8 at 2" x 2" - A
  64 at 1 1/4" x 1 1/4" - E

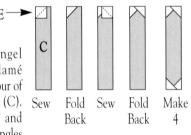

1. Vertical rows between angel blocks: Sew two 1 1/4" lamé squares (E) to each end of four of the 2" x 10 1/2" navy strips (C). Squares are sewn "double" and folded back to finish as triangles for points of gold stars.

Sew   Fold Back   Sew   Fold Back   Make 4

2. Construct horizontal center row of wallhanging as follows: plain piece C, piece C with star points, *piece D, piece C with star points.* Repeat between asterisks two more times and end by adding a plain piece C.

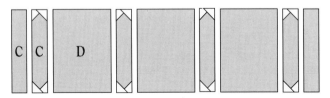

3. Horizontal star rows: Sew two 1 1/4" lamé squares (E) to each end of six of the 2" x 7 1/2" navy strips (B). Squares are folded to become triangles as in step 1.

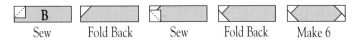

Sew   Fold Back   Sew   Fold Back   Make 6

4. Horizontal star rows, continued: Sew two 1 1/4" lamé squares (E) to one side of four of the 2" navy squares (A).  Make 4

A   E

5. Construct two horizontal star rows as follows: navy square A with star points, lamé square A, *piece B with star points, lamé square A.* Repeat between asterisks two more times and end by adding a navy square A with star points.

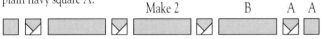

A   A   B

6. Top and bottom rows: Sew two 1 1/4" lamé squares (E) to one side of eight of the 2" navy squares (A).  Make 8

A   E

7. Construct top and bottom rows as follows: plain navy square A, navy square A with star points, *plain navy strip B, navy square A with star points.* Repeat between asterisks two more times and end by adding a plain navy square A.

Make 2   B   A   A

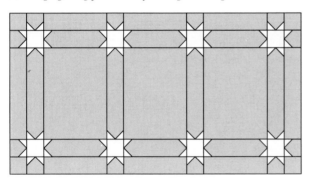

8. Sew star rows and top and bottom rows to center horizontal row of wallhanging using photo and quilt diagram as a guide. Press well.

9. Angels: Make template of wing, dress, head, arm, scallop, and stars for halo, page 23. Using templates, trace patterns onto smooth, paper side of fusing web. Remember to trace two arms with one reversed. Trace 3 large stars and 12 small ones.

10. Press fusing web to **wrong** side of desired fabric with rough side facing fabric. Cut out shapes. With pencil, lightly transfer face markings. Peel off paper. Position angels on 7" x 10" blocks on wallhanging centering them from left to right and having them about 1" from bottom of block. Lay down wings first then head and arms. Lay down dress lapping it over raw edges of neck and arms. Lay down scallops on dress and stars for hair/halo. Press in place. Use photo as a guide.

11. Using permanent marking pens, draw eyes in brown and mouth in red. Use side of red pencil lead to blush cheeks or use powder blush.

12. Cut backing and batting 18" x 32". Layer backing wrong side up, then batting, and then top right side up. Baste. Quilt as desired. Wallhanging in photo was machine quilted in the ditch around the angel blocks only. Trim batting and backing even with top.

13. Cut three strips of binding 2 1/2" x width of fabric. Bind wallhanging referring to step 14 of Calico and Buttons Angel Quilt, page 4.

14. Hang banner on wall with sequin pins or attach 1" plastic rings to back for hanging.

ANGEL GREETING CARD

(5 1/2" x 8 1/2") Pictured on page 15.

Yardage and Supplies
Fabric (42" - 45"):
*   Head and arms - scrap at least 4 1/2" square*
*   Dress - scrap at least 6" square*
*   Wings - scrap at least 3 1/2" x 5 1/2"*
*   Trees - scrap at least 3" x 6"*
Paper-backed fusing web - 1/6 yard
Fine permanent marking pens - red and brown
Red pencil or powder blush
Glitter paint such as Tulip Paint Writer - gold
Permanent gold marking pen for writing letter
Purchased stationery or heavy paper (8 1/2" x 11") and envelope to fit folded card (approximately 5 1/2" x 8 1/2").

To Make Greeting Card:
1. Fold 8 1/2" x 11" stationery in half to form a card 5 1/2" x 8 1/2".
2. Make templates for wing, head, arm, trees, and dress, page 23.
3. Using templates, trace patterns onto smooth, paper side of fusing web. Remember to trace two arms with one reversed.
4. Press fusing web to **wrong** side of desired fabric with rough side facing fabric. Cut out shapes. With pencil, lightly transfer face markings.
5. Peel off paper; position angel dress approximately 1/2" from bottom of card front. Layer remaining angel pieces sliding wing, head, and arms under dress. Overlap raw edges of head and arms with dress. When design is pleasing, press in place.
6. Using permanent marking pens, draw eyes in brown and mouth in red. Use side of red pencil lead to blush cheeks or use powder blush.
7. To make halo/hair, use glitter paint and make a zig-zag line from ear level on one side of head to ear level on other side.
8. In pencil lightly draw "JOY" on top part of card. Then go over it with glitter paint.
9. Send the card to someone special!

GLITTER AND GLOW ANGEL

(10" x 13") Pictured on page 11.

Yardage and Supplies
Fabric (42" - 45"):
*   Head and arms - scrap at least 4 1/2" square*
*   Dress - 5 to 6 different scraps at least 3" x 6"*
*   Wings - 5" or 6" lace doily*
*   Stars - gold lamé scrap at least 6" square*
*   Background fabric - 16" x 18" or 1/2 yard*
Fine permanent marking pens - red and brown
Red pencil or powder blush
Gold oval picture frame approximately 13" x 16" with a 10" x 13" opening
Glitter paint such as Tulip Paint Writer - gold
Adhesive glitter such as Glitterstik - gold
Gold cording 1/16" wide - 1/2 yard (to outline dress)
Laces and ribbons - 5 to 6 small pieces
Paper-backed fusing web - 1/6 yard
Template plastic
Thick, tacky glue

To Make Angel:

1. Make templates of angel dress pieces, head, arms, and star page 24.
2. Trace patterns onto smooth, paper side of fusing web. **Trace dress shapes the reverse of the direction wanted.** Remember to trace two arms with one reversed. Press fusing web to **wrong** side of desired fabric with rough side facing fabric. Cut out shapes. Lightly transfer face markings with a pencil. Trace and cut out 13 stars.
3. Peel off paper. Position angel with head in center of background fabric.
4. Layer in this order: doily, head, arms. Lap dress over neck and arm edges. Add stars. When the arrangement is pleasing, press. Note: Angel head and arms may be double-layered to prevent show-through.
5. Cover edges of dress sections with lace and ribbon pieces. Glue into place with tacky glue.
6. Using permanent making pens, draw mouth in red and eyes in brown. Use side of red pencil lead to blush cheeks or use powder blush. Use the brown pen to outline arms.
7. Glue gold cording around outer edge of dress.
8. To make hair/halo, use glitter paint and make zig-zag line from ear level on one side of head to ear level on other side.
9. Use Glitterstik in areas between stars. Embellish lace, stars, and background with glitter paint as shown in photo.
10. Frame the angel yourself or have it professionally framed. Hang and enjoy!

ANGELS GALORE SWEATSHIRT

Pictured on pages 9 and 13.
Yardage and Supplies
Fabric (42" - 45"):
  Head and arms - scrap at least 4 1/2" square
  Dress - scrap at least 6" square
  Wings and stars - lamé of desired color - 1/8 yard
Paper-backed fusing web - 1/6 yard
Fine permanent marking pens - brown and red
Red pencil or powder blush
Adhesive glitter such as Glitterstik - gold
Glitter paint such as Tulip Paint Writer - gold
Template plastic
Sweatshirt of desired color and size (adult or child)

To Decorate Sweatshirt:

1. To find center front line of sweatshirt, fold it in half matching side and shoulder seams. Press lightly. Use this pressed line as a placement guide. Set sweatshirt aside.
2. Make templates of wing, dress, head, arm, and star, page 23.
3. Using templates, trace patterns onto smooth, paper side of fusing web. Remember to trace two arms with one reversed. Trace 18 stars.
4. Press fusing web to **wrong** side of desired fabric with rough side facing fabric. Cut out shapes. With pencil, lightly transfer face markings.
5. Peel off paper; position top of angel head 4 1/2" down from sweatshirt neck edge along center front crease line. Lay wings down and slip slightly under head and neck edges. Position arms and lay dress on top to cover neck and arm edges. When the design is pleasing, press in place.
6. Referring to photo, arrange stars as desired. Press.
7. Using permanent marking pens, draw eyes in brown and mouth in red.

Use side of red pencil lead to blush cheeks or use powder blush.

8. To make halo/hair, use glitter paint and make zig-zag line from ear level on one side of head to ear level on other side.
9. With same paint, outline wings and add some extra texture lines on wings. If desired, the pattern design of the dress fabric may be embellished with the glitter paint. Also the stars may be outlined with the glitter paint. Allow to dry.
10. Follow manufacturer's directions for Glitterstik. Apply Glitterstik to the outer edges of all stars. Allow to dry thoroughly. Your sweatshirt is now ready to wear.
11. To launder sweatshirt, either hand wash or machine wash on gentle cycle with shirt turned wrong side out. When ironing, cover design area with a presscloth. If any of the glitter has come off, reapply where needed.
12. Enjoy wearing your holiday sweatshirt!

DECORATED BAND BOX

(14" diameter) Pictured on page 13.
Yardage and Supplies
*Purchased, ready-made band box, **or** band box kit, **or** Keepsake Sampler Box Kit, or Keepsake Sampler pattern #165. Keepsake Sampler pattern and Keepsake Sampler Box Kit are available from **Possibilities.** Catalog available; address and phone number are on back cover. Keepsake Box Kit was used to make box in photo.*
Box fabric - use requirements given for specific box kit or pattern
Angel fabric (42" - 45"):
  Head and arms - scrap at least 4 1/2" square
  Dress - scrap at least 6" square
  Wings - scrap at least 3 1/2" x 5 1/2"
Paper-backed fusing web - 1/6 yard
Fine permanent marking pens - brown and red
Red pencil or powder blush
Glitter paint such as Tulip Paint Writer - gold
Glue gun and glue sticks or thick, tacky glue
Gold star garland - 2 yards
1" gold sequin snowflakes - 14
Template plastic

To Make Decorated Band Box:

1. Purchase or make band box according to manufacturer's directions. Set aside.
2. Make templates of wing, dress, head, and arm, page 23.
3. Using templates, trace patterns onto smooth, paper side of fusing web. Remember to trace two arms with one reversed.
4. Press fusing web to **wrong** side of desired fabric with rough side facing fabric. Cut out shapes. With pencil, lightly transfer face markings.
5. Peel off paper. Layer and position angel pieces on top of band box having neck edge of angel a little above center (half-way mark) of lid. Refer to photo. Layer angel parts in the following order: wings first, then head, then arms in down position, and then dress. Dress overlaps neck and arm edges. Press in place. If necessary, put a book or something sturdy under the box lid to support the weight of the iron.
6. Using fine permanent marking pens, draw eyes in brown and mouth in red. Use side of red pencil lead to blush cheeks or use powder blush.
7. To make halo/hair, use glitter paint to make zig-zag line from ear level on one side of head to ear level on other side. Outline wings with glitter paint. Continue on page 17.

HALLELUJAH ANGEL PICTURE, page 18

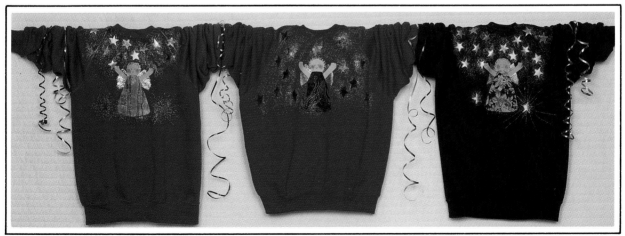

ANGELS GALORE SWEATSHIRT, page 8

FANCY APRON AND STRING OF STARS TREE SKIRT, page 17
CHRISTMAS STOCKING, page 4

STAINED ANGEL CHEESE BOX, page 5

GLITTER AND GLOW ANGEL, page 7

GLITZY GIFT BAG, page 18

TRIO OF ANGELS BANNER, page 6

PAINTED ANGEL COOKIE TRAY, page 19

ANGEL WRAPPING PAPER, page 4

PAINTED ANGEL IN GRAPEVINE WREATH, page 3

MEMORIES PHOTO ALBUM COVER, page 2

ANGELS GALORE SWEATSHIRT, page 8

DECORATED BAND BOX, page 8

HOMESPUN CHRISTMAS WALLHANGING, page 19

RUFFLED PILLOW, page 5

ANGEL STATIONERY AND ENVELOPE, page 18

ANGEL GREETING CARD, page 7

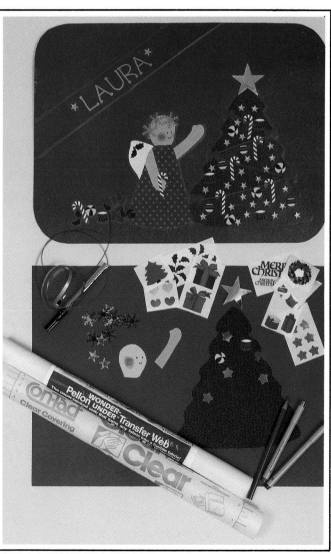

TRIM-A-TREE PLACEMAT, page 3

CALICO AND BUTTONS
ANGEL QUILT, page 4

Nancy Smith and Lynda Milligan are founders of the Denver-based retail
store *Great American Quilt Factory, Inc.* They also manufacture a line of
patterns called *DreamSpinners*. These patterns are for soft goods including
quilts, dolls, teddy bears, decorative items, and clothing. Smith and
Milligan also own and operate *Possibilities* which at the present time
publishes quilt and other craft-related books. For a full color catalog of
available products, please send $2 to:

Great American Quilt Factory, Inc.
8970 East Hampden Avenue
Denver, Colorado 80231

Phone: 303-740-6206
Fax: 303-220-7424

8. On top of box, arrange and glue 14 snowflakes as shown in photo. Use either glue gun or tacky glue.
9. Cut a 9" piece of star garland. Glue one end of garland to each angel hand as shown.
10. Glue garland around outside of band box. From top of box measure 3" down one corner and glue garland end to this mark. Drape garland around box gluing into same position at each corner. Garland should drape to about 3" from base of box.
11. Allow to thoroughly dry.
12. Use your special box to tuck away holiday treasures.

STRING OF STARS TREE SKIRT

(47" diameter) Pictured on page 10.
Yardage and Supplies
Fabric (42" - 45"):
  Tree skirt top and back - 2 1/2 yards (or 1 1/4 yards each)
  Ruffle and angel wings - 2 yards
  Head and arms - 1/8 yard
  Dresses - 3/8 yard
Low-loft batting - 45" square
Paper-backed fusing web - 1 yard
Gold star garland - 4 yards
Glitter paint such as Tulip Paint Writer - gold
Fine permanent marking pens - red and brown
Red pencil or powder blush
Thread to match tree skirt fabric
Template plastic
Glue gun and glue sticks or thick, tacky glue

To Make Tree Skirt:
(Use 1/4" seam allowance unless otherwise noted.)
1. Begin by cutting a 42" circle for the top of the tree skirt. To do this, cut a 44" square from the skirt top fabric. Fold square in half, then fold in half again. Now fold diagonally out from center. Press well. You now have eight equally divided sections. To mark circle for outside edge of tree skirt, place a tape measure on exact center point of folded, pressed tree skirt top. Measure out 21" and make a small pencil mark. Hold tape measure end at center and swing it around marking 21" at 1" to 2" intervals. Cut on this marked arc. You should now have a 42" circle with eight pressed divisions. Cut a 44" square of fabric for tree skirt back. Set aside while preparing eight angels.

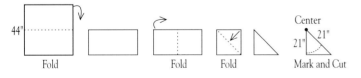

2. Make templates for wing, head, arm, and dress, page 23.
3. Using templates, trace patterns onto smooth, paper side of fusing web. Remember to trace two arms with one reversed for each angel.
4. Press fusing web to **wrong** side of desired fabric with rough side facing fabric. Cut out shapes. With pencil, lightly transfer face markings.
5. Peel off paper; position each of the eight angels along a pressed crease line having bottom of angel dress approximately 1 1/2" from outside edge of tree skirt. Lay wings down then head. Position arms (every other angel has arms placed in down position). Lay dress on top overlapping neck and arm edges. When the design is pleasing, press in place.

6. Using permanent marking pens, draw eyes in brown and mouth in red. Use side of red pencil lead to blush cheeks or use powder blush.
7. To make halo/hair, use glitter paint and make a zig-zag line from ear level on one side of head to ear level on other side.
8. On wrong side of tree skirt top, lightly draw a 5" circle at the center. Mark one line for back slit from circle to outside edge centered between two angels.
9. To prepare ruffle, cut nine strips of fabric 6 1/2" wide by width of fabric. Seam ends of strips together to make one long, continuous strip. Press 1/2" to wrong side on each end. Press strip in half lengthwise right side out. Run two rows of gathering stitches along raw edges inside the 1/4" seam allowance. Fold ruffle into eighths (i.e., halves, quarters, eighths) and mark eighth points. With right sides together and raw edges even, pin ruffle to outer edge of tree skirt top; place each end 3/8" from marked line for back slit (line is marked on wrong side). Pin one-eighth ruffle markings into position halfway between angels. Pull up gathers and baste ruffle in place.

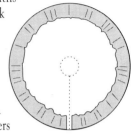

10. Lay batting on a flat surface. Lay the wrong side of tree skirt backing square on top of batting. Lay the right side of tree skirt top onto the right side of the backing. Pin or baste into place. Trim away extra batting and backing.
11. Stitch 1/4" from each side of mark for back slit leaving an 8" to 10" opening; stitch on marked circle for center hole; stitch just inside basting that attached ruffle at outside edge of tree skirt. Cut on mark between stitching lines at back slit; cut away excess at center circle 1/4" from stitching line. Clip seam at center.

Leave open

12. Turn tree skirt right side out through opening. Press carefully using a presscloth, if necessary, over angels.
13. Tuck in raw edges of opening and slipstitch closed.
14. Using picture as a guide, drape star garland over angels and tack or glue into place.
15. Place under Christmas tree and enjoy!

FANCY APRON

(One size) Pictured on page 10.
Yardage and Supplies
Fabric (42" - 45"):
  Apron - 1 5/8 yards
  Head and arms - scrap at least 4 1/2" square
  Dress - scrap at least 6" square
  Wings - scrap at least 3 1/2" x 5 1/2"
Paper-backed fusing web - 1/4 yard
Fine permanent marking pens - red and brown
Red pencil or powder blush
Glitter paint such as Tulip Paint Writer - gold
Thread to match apron fabric
Gold star garland - 7"

To Make Apron:

(Use 1/2" seam allowance unless otherwise noted.)
1. Cut: 1 skirt - 24" x 42"
   2 bibs - 9" x 10 1/2"
   1 waistband - 3 3/4" x 14 3/4"
   2 waistband ties - 3 3/4" x 30 1/2"
   2 neck ties - 3 3/4 " x 27 1/2"
2. Narrowly hem one long and two short edges of skirt; gather remaining long edge.
3. Sew one short end of each waistband tie to each short end of waistband right sides together.
4. Pull up gathered edge of skirt to fit waistband. Pin right sides together and stitch. Press in 1/2" on all remaining raw edges of waistband and waistband ties.
5. Make bib and neck ties. Fold each neck tie in half lengthwise right sides together; stitch long edge and one short end leaving other short end open to turn.  Turn; press. With right sides together, pin ties to one 9" side of bib 1/2" from side edges; baste. With right sides together, pin bib facing to bib. Stitch top and side edges catching in ends of neck ties. Trim corners; turn; press.
6. Center and pin bottom raw edge of bib right sides together on free edge of waistband; sew in place.
7. Fold waistband and waistband ties lengthwise wrong sides together and pin in place from right side of apron. Fold bib up into its finished position and pin in place. Topstitch catching bib in topstitching at top edge of waistband. Hint: Start stitching at lower edge of waistband.
8. Cut, bond, and embellish angel with arms in down position following steps 2 through 7 of String of Stars Tree Skirt on page 17 omitting references to angel placement. Use photo as guide for placement.
9. Cut a 7" piece of star garland and glue or tack into place between angel's hands.
10. Enjoy wearing your holiday apron!

HALLELUJAH ANGEL PICTURE

(11" x 15") Pictured on page 9.

Yardage and Supplies
Fabric (42" - 45"):
   Head and arms - scrap at least 4 1/2" square
   Dress - scrap at least 6" square
   Wings - scrap at least 3 1/2" x 5 1/2"
   Trees - scrap at least 3" x 6"
   Stars - lamé scrap at least 6" square
   Background - 14" x 18" or 1/2 yard
Paper-backed fusing web - 1/4 yard
Fine permanent marking pens - red and brown
Red pencil or powder blush
Glitter paint such as Tulip Paint Writer - gold
Template plastic
Red frame and picture glass - 11" x 15" - or have picture professionally framed

To Make Picture:
1. Cut a piece of background fabric 14" x 18". Fold fabric in half

vertically and then horizontally. Fingerpress creases. These are placement guidelines for angel.
2. Make templates of wing, dress, head, arm, two sizes of stars, and tree section, page 23.
3. Using templates, trace patterns onto smooth, paper side of fusing web. Remember to trace two arms with one reversed. Trace six small stars and eight large stars.
4. Press fusing web to **wrong** side of desired fabric with rough side facing fabric. Cut out shapes. With pencil, lightly transfer face markings. Peel off paper.
5. Lay background fabric on table with 14" sides at top and bottom. Place angel head at center of background fabric. Lay wings down and slip slightly under head and neck edges. Position arms and lay dress on top to cover neck and arm edges. Position trees as shown near bottom of dress. When the design is pleasing, press in place.
6. Referring to photo, arrange stars as desired. Press.
7. Using permanent marking pens, draw eyes in brown and mouth in red. Use side of red pencil lead to blush cheeks or use powder blush.
8. To make halo/hair, use glitter paint to make zig-zag line from ear level on one side of head to ear level on other side.
9. Press background to remove guideline creases.
10. Either frame picture according to frame manufacturer's directions or have it professionally framed. Hang and enjoy!

ANGEL STATIONERY AND ENVELOPE

Pictured on page 15.

Yardage and Supplies   *Purchased stationery*
Fabric (42" - 45"):
   Head and arms - scrap of fabric at least 4 1/2" square
   Dress - scrap of fabric at least 6" square
   Wings - scrap at least 3 1/2" x 5 1/2"
   Stars - scrap of gold lamé at least 2" x 4"
Paper-backed fusing web - 1/6 yard
Fine permanent marking pens - red and brown
Red pencil or powder blush
Glitter paint such as Tulip Paint Writer - gold
Template plastic

To Make Stationery and Envelope:
1. Make templates for wing, head, arm, dress, and star, page 22.
2. Follow steps 3 through 7 for Angel Greeting Card on page 7, omitting trees on dress.
3. Position one star along side of dress and one star along left side of envelope. Press. Refer to photo for approximate placement.
4. With glitter paint, draw lines radiating out from stars. Allow to dry thoroughly.
5. Enjoy writing a letter to someone special!

GLITZY GIFT BAG

(8" x 10" x 4 1/2") Pictured on page 11.

Yardage and Supplies
Fabric (42" - 45"):
   Head and arms - scrap at least 4 1/2" square
   Dress - scrap at least 6" square
   Wings and stars - gold lamé scrap at least 4" x 9"
Paper-backed fusing web - 1/6 yard
Fine permanent marking pens - brown and red

Red pencil or powder blush
Glitter paint such as Tulip Paint Writer - gold
Template plastic
Gift bag approximately 8" x 10"

To Make Gift Bag:

1. Refer to steps 2 through 8 for Angels Galore Sweatshirt, page 8, using smaller star and omitting references to sweatshirt. If necessary, use a presscloth when ironing onto bag.
2. Outline angel dress, head, and wings with gold glitter paint and add extra texture lines along wings.
3. Either have a florist fill bag with floral arrangement or do it yourself. Use your gift bag as a fireplace or table decoration.

HOMESPUN CHRISTMAS WALLHANGING

(20" x 24") Pictured on page 14.

Yardage and Supplies

Fabric (42" - 45"):
  Background - 5/8 yard
  Border, binding, tabs - 5/8 yard
  Backing - 3/4 yard
  Tree - scraps of greens (homespuns, country prints) at least 4" x 8", scrap of brown 2" x 2"
  Gifts - scraps of greens and reds at least 3" x 3"
  Star - scrap of cream homespun at least 2 1/2" x 2 1/2"
Paper-backed fusing web - 1/2 yard
Low-loft batting - 2/3 yard
Ribbon - scraps of assorted color and design (for gifts)
Embellishments such as tiny jingle bells, star sequins (for gifts)
Embroidery floss - DMC #355 (for button garland)
Buttons - tan, cream, brown (for button garland)
Wood beads - 1/8" - red, cream (for button garland)
Ceramic star button (for top of tree)
Thread to match border/binding and background
Thick, tacky glue
Liquid fray preventer
Brass curtain rod (optional)

To Make Wallhanging:

(Use 1/4" seam allowance unless otherwise noted.)

1. Cut background 16" x 20".
2. Trace tree pattern pieces, page 22, onto smooth side of fusing web (this will create a mirror image of the design). Bond each tree piece to desired fabric (rough side of fusing web to **wrong** side of fabric). Cut out; peel off paper backing. Arrange on background centered from left to right with tree trunk 4 3/4" from bottom edge. Bond into place. Bond homespun star into place 1/4" above treetop.
3. Bond scraps for gifts with fusing web and cut out ten various sizes of squares and rectangles (examples: 1 1/4" x 1 3/4 ", 1 1/2" x 2", 2" x 2"). Using photo as a guide, bond gifts in an arc under the tree.
4. Button garland: Using photo as a guide for placement, sew buttons to wallhanging using six strands of embroidery floss. Sew on one button at at time finishing with a square knot on the top of the button. Leave 1/8" "tails" and secure knot with liquid fray preventer. Sew wooden beads between buttons. Sew ceramic star button to homespun star with a square knot as before.
5. Gift embellishments: Use thick, tacky glue to secure ribbons, bells, sequins, and beads to gifts.

6. Cut two side borders 2 1/2" x 20 1/2". Cut two top/bottom borders 2 1/2" x 16 1/2". Cut four corners (from gift fabrics) 2 1/2" x 2 1/2".
7. Sew side borders to wallhanging. Sew corner gifts to each end of top and bottom borders. Sew top and bottom borders to wallhanging. Press seams toward border.
8. Cut backing and batting 2" bigger on each side than wallhanging top. Layer backing right side down, then batting, then wallhanging top right side up. Baste.
9. Hand or machine quilt 1/4" from edges of tree and star. Quilt in the ditch between background and border.
10. Embellish gifts in four corners.
11. Cut four strips for binding 2 1/2" x width of fabric. Bind wallhanging referring to step 14 of Calico and Buttons Angel Quilt.
12. Tabs: Cut strip of border/binding fabric 2 1/2" x 25". Fold in half lengthwise right sides together and stitch 1/4" from long raw edges. Turn tube right side out and cut into five segments. Fold each segment in half with seam inside. Tucking in raw edges, hand stitch at evenly spaced intervals to top edge of wallhanging on back. See photo.
13. Hang from curtain rod and enjoy!

PAINTED ANGEL COOKIE TRAY

(10" x 13") Pictured on page 12.

Supplies

Unpainted tray approximately 10" x 13"
Acrylic paints:
  Folk Art Icy White - background
  Folk Art Skintone - face and arms
  Folk Art Parrot Green - trees
  Delta Ceramcoat Maroon - dress, cheeks, back of tray
  Accent Summersand #2501 - wings
  DecoArt Glorious Gold - stars
Synthetic brushes in several small sizes for applying paint
Small, stiff brush for applying cheeks
McCloskey's Wood Sealer
Small polyfoam brush for applying sealer
Fine permanent marking pen - brown - Niji or Pigma
Tracing paper
Graphite transfer paper (gray)
Drafting tape to hold pattern in place

To Decorate Cookie Tray:

1. Sand tray. Seal with wood sealer.
2. Paint tray white on front and maroon on back and sides. Let dry.
3. Trace pattern from book, page 20, onto tracing paper. Transfer pattern to tray using graphite transfer paper (used the same way as carbon paper).
4. Paint angel starting with face and arms. Then paint wings and dress. Paint trees and stars last.
5. Use permanent pen to outline angel and add details such as lines on wings, face, and halo. See photo.
6. Use small, stiff brush to apply cheeks using the dry brush technique. Dab brush in maroon paint and then dab on paper towel to remove most of the paint. Test before using by pouncing on towel; apply to cheeks by pouncing lightly.
7. Seal tray with wood sealer.
8. Pile your tray with holiday treats!

Stars and Moon
for Ruffled Pillow

RUFFLED PILLOW
PAINTED ANGEL COOKIE TRAY
STAINED ANGEL CHEESE BOX

Star for
Painted Angel
Cookie Tray

20

Centerline - Make Template Full Size

HOMESPUN
CHRISTMAS WALLHANGING

22

Stars for Trio of Angels Banner
and Glitzy Gift Bag

Stars for
all Others

TRIO OF ANGELS BANNER
GLITZY GIFT BAG
STRING OF STARS TREE SKIRT
FANCY APRON
CHRISTMAS STOCKING
MEMORIES PHOTO ALBUM COVER
ANGEL CREETING CARD
ANGELS GALORE SWEATSHIRT
ANGEL WRAPPING PAPER
HALLELUJAH ANGEL PICTURE
CALICO AND BUTTONS ANGEL QUILT
DECORATED BAND BOX

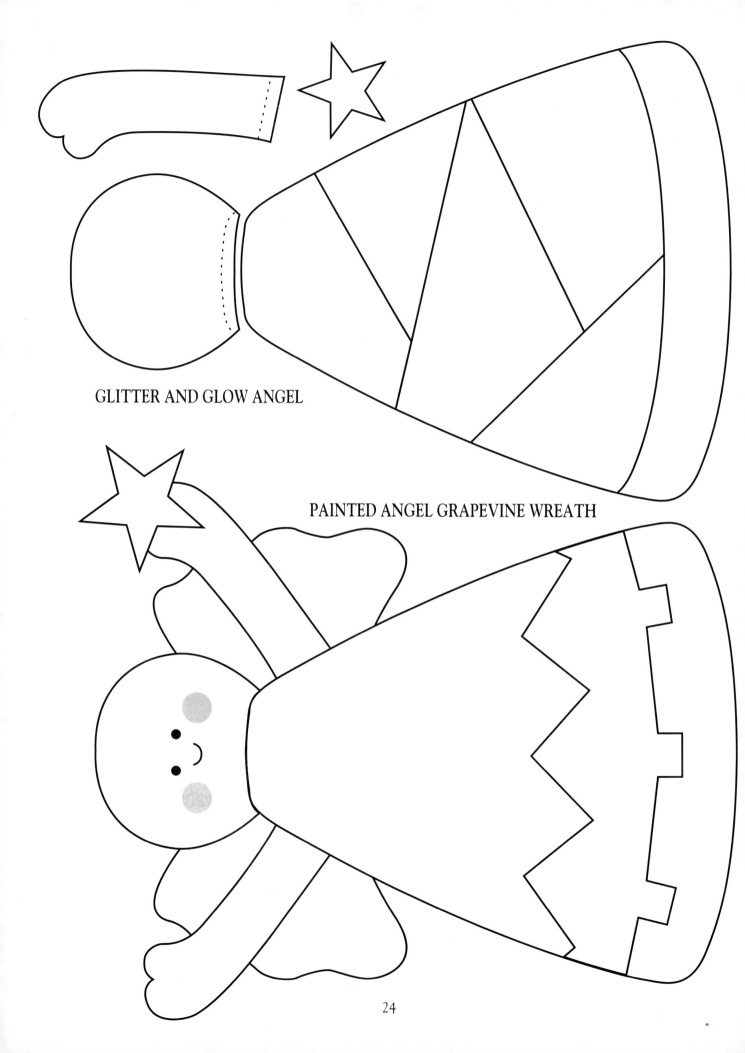

GLITTER AND GLOW ANGEL

PAINTED ANGEL GRAPEVINE WREATH

24